CUBE*chic*

TAKE YOUR OFFICE SPACE FROM **DRAB** TO **FAB!**

by *Kelley L. Moore*

QUIRK BOOKS

PHILADELPHIA

Library of Congress Cataloging in Publication Number: 2005934382

ISBN: 1-59474-105-0

Manufactured in China

Cube Chic: Take Your Office Space from Drab to Fab is produced by becker&mayer!, Bellevue, Washington
www.beckermayer.com

Cubicle Design and Style: Kelley L. Moore
Book Layout and Design: Todd Bates
Editorial: Kate Perry and Adrienne Wiley
Production Coordination: Adrian Lucia
Project Management: Sheila Kamuda

Distributed in North America by Chronicle Books
85 Second Street
San Francisco, CA 94105

10 9 8 7 6 5 4 3 2 1

Quirk Books
215 Church Street
Philadelphia, PA 19106
www.quirkbooks.com

INTRODUCTION

There's no doubt that someday you'll have a corner office with your name on the door, but in the meantime, don't settle for less just because your desk is standard issue. You're not a featureless, same-as-the-next-guy entity. Why should your cube be?

Every living and working space contains amazing potential when viewed with a combination of imagination and energy, the same blend that leads to business success. The beleaguered work cubicle, the subject of so many jokes, presents a proverbial blank canvas. If you can transform the three walls of your work area into a space reminiscent of Studio 54 or your favorite golf course, then you're almost certain to have what it takes to move up from your cubicle to an office with a window.

The materials required to create the cubes shown in this book vary, and some materials are easier and less time consuming to work with than others. Here are a few tips to consider before you begin:

- When using hot glue to secure a material to your desk, shelves, or cubical walls, place a strong, clear adhesive tape along the perimeter of the area first, and apply the hot glue on top of the tape to prevent damage to the office furniture. When you tear down one creation to work on the next, remove the tape and apply a new strip.

- Vinyl is the least forgiving of the materials we suggest you work with. If you have to store the vinyl prior to using it, lay it out flat, as it will crease if you fold it. If you have to fold it to store, use a hair dryer to remove any creases: With the hair dryer approximately 12 inches (36 cm) from the vinyl, blow the hot air along the crease to warm the vinyl until the crease disappears. Velcro stuck to the back of vinyl will cause it to buckle, so straight pins and tacks are your best tools when hanging it on your walls. Be aware that straight pins or tacks will leave a hole in the vinyl if you have to take them out and reposition them.

- Felt and corrugated paper are easy to work with and quick to hang. If you use hot glue to attach trim to these materials, be aware that removing the trim will tear the corrugated paper and leave an impression on the felt.

- Clear vinyl makes a good writing surface if you're covering your desk with a textured material.

- The Resources section on page 94 lists you where you can purchase the materials and accessories used in each cubicle design.

Now let your imagination run wild! *Cube Chic* offers twenty-two ideas for taking the "square" out of your cube—from old Hollywood glamour to the comfort of a cozy pub, from the Big Apple to the Garden of Eden. Explore these themes, and add a dash of your self-styled glitz to put on the Ritz or discover your jungle boogie, be it on the dance floor or on safari. Whether you're surrounded by bling or in a backwoods cabin, you'll discover that working in a cubicle isn't so bad after all!

*safari*CUBE

 **F**or two centuries, the allure of the safari has drawn adventurers from every continent to explore the mysteries of the African landscape. Sir Richard Burton spent a lifetime describing his travels along the Nile, through the savannah, and into the jungle. The nineteenth-century explorer would extricate himself from certain death time and again, only to return to another perilous destination mere months later. Creating a visual celebration of the wilds of Africa is a more pedestrian affair to be sure, but perhaps just the right design scheme will inspire your next vacation.

Adding patterns of the savannah, especially cheetah print, will guarantee a wild tone, and African masks, totems, or other pieces are excellent (and readily available) for adding authenticity to your cubescape. Handsome desktop accessories, including the ubiquitous mosquito netting, complete your jungle getaway. Remember your pith helmet and bush knife—you're going to need them!

Bring out the animal within using cheetah print, feathers, and fur trim.

project: NATURAL WALLS

MATERIALS:

- Natural burlap
- Straight pins
- Capiz shell curtains
- Scissors
- Wooden stick
- Feather strands
- Hot glue gun
- Hot glue
- Large piece of faux fur fabric

1. Secure the natural burlap to the cubicle walls with straight pins at the top, bottom, and along the sides. You shouldn't have to piece the burlap together because it can be bought in panels wide enough to cover the entire wall.

2. Purchase capiz shell curtains at a home goods store and cut each strand so you are left with several individual strands of shells. Trim each strand to match the height of your cubicle wall and hot glue the strands, spaced about 6 inches (15 cm) apart, to a wooden stick.

3. Hang the wooden stick at the top of the wall, and secure to the wall with hot glue.

4. Hot glue feather strands around the top edge of the burlap.

5. Cut 1-inch (2.5 cm) strips from the large piece of faux fur fabric and use hot glue to apply a fur trim to the bottom edge of the burlap on the base of each cubicle wall.

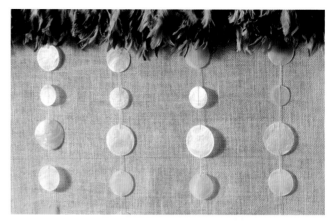

Once you create your natural walls, the beautiful capiz shells will reflect light and the feathers will add texture.

WALLS

■ Natural texture is the focus for the cubicle walls. Create the background with natural burlap held in place with straight pins. Add a bit of shine to the matte burlap with a layer of capiz shells. The wall can then be trimmed in mixed feathers and faux fur to add a primitive ingredient to the overall look. See the project to the left for tips on how to layer these elements.

■ Shelves can also be covered in a natural burlap. Trim the shelves in faux fur to coordinate with the cubicle walls. Hold both the burlap and faux fur in place with hot glue. (For tips on working with hot glue, see page 5.)

DESK

■ Master business negotiations by following your animal instincts: Cover your desk in leopard-print vinyl, securing it underneath with duct tape. (For tips on working with vinyl, see page 5.)

■ Hot glue strips of faux fur to the edge of the desk to soften the texture of the vinyl.

The jungle will be jumpin' when you put a photograph of your favorite animal in a simple picture frame.

Roaming wooden giraffes add character to your celebration of the thrill of the hunt.

DÉCOR

■ Create a jungle inside your cube by placing a faux banana tree to one side of the entrance and adding a faux fern or a large aloe plant in a corner.

■ You don't have to be a hunter to include an animal pelt in your design. Find a faux fur or a fabric with an animal skin print to imitate the look and feel of the wild. Place your pelt on the floor or drape it over a chair or filing cabinet for maximum impact.

■ If you don't have a collection of African masks or statues from your last trip to Cape Town, visit your local international goods store and you're sure to find a nice selection. The dark wood will play off of the natural burlap to add an exotic cast to your cube.

■ Hand-carved statues of elephants and giraffes nestled amid binders and books make for a welcome surprise.

■ A wooden box adorned with a hand-carved African landscape is an elegant place to store your office supplies.

■ A small lamp with an amber-tinted shade will cast a subtle glow, transforming your space from mundane to mysterious with the push of a button.

■ Hang a mosquito net over your cubical to inspire daydreams of lounging in an oversized bed with crisp white linens while listening to tropical birds.

*garden*CUBE

 Gardening provides a chance to appreciate natural beauty. Surrounded by a variety of flowers and plants, we breathe more easily and see life in a different light. In the garden cube, your environment will overflow with fluorescent light–loving flora as you invite your colleagues to visit your personal Eden.

Add fresh-cut flowers each Monday to bring dazzle to your work week. An assortment of ceramic pots in themes or like colors will bring the earthy, natural scent of gardening indoors. (Leave plants potted in plastic inside the pots to keep things neat.) Select containers in the mustard hues of Tuscany, or plant flowers in teapots—there's no limit to the planter possibilities! Statues are conversation pieces as well as reflections of your personality: Bypass formality and add some kitsch with a hidden gnome here and a troll there to lighten up the space. Leather stationery accessories and candles scented with rose garden or freshly mown grass aromas will inspire you as you toil at the keyboard without ever leaving the garden!

Bring the sunshine inside to inspire fresh ideas and thoughts of greener pastures.

WALLS

■ Designing a background for your garden cube is as easy as fastening sheets of faux plastic grass to the walls with straight pins. If you can't find faux grass at a craft or party store, Astroturf will work, but it's more difficult to secure to the walls and provides a heavier look.

■ To add a romantic touch, trim the top of the walls with silk wisteria. Use straight pins to attach several garlands of wisteria as high as you can on the cubicle walls.

DESK

■ Whether you want your garden structured and modern or wild and romantic, cover the desk with a material that blends with the color of the silk flowers you select to adorn the cube. Floral chintz fabrics or pastel cotton prints are good options. Cut the fabric to fit the top of the desk (with extra material to secure underneath), pull it tight, and secure it with duct tape along the edges.

■ Trim the desk in a 2-inch-wide (5 cm) gingham ribbon for a country look, or choose a vibrant color that complements the overall color palette of your garden for a more modern approach. The ribbon should be wrapped around the edge and secured to the top and bottom of the fabric with a thin line of hot glue. (For tips on working with hot glue, see page 5.)

DÉCOR

■ A cobblestone path is a unique way to cover the cubicle floor. Buy corrugated paper printed with cobblestones, and cut the stones out of the paper. Leave a very thin outline of black

from the imprint around the cobblestone to add definition. Arrange the cobblestones with about a ½-inch (1.3 cm) of floor showing and stick the paper to the floor with double-sided tape to keep them in place even when trod upon. Adding circles of Astroturf provides an area for "planting."

■ Fresh flowers bring life to your work space. A miniature birdbath is an ideal place to nestle your favorite fresh flower. Silk flowers are a more lasting decoration; for a high-end look, arrange them in a monotone palette, mixing various shades of a single color.

■ To mimic the look of a European garden, à la Versailles, add a silk topiary tree (shown to the left) to your cubicle.

■ A wicker chair with a bright-colored throw under a garden umbrella will transport your guests to an outdoor Eden.

■ Statues of a dog digging in the dirt, an oversized mushroom, or a garden gnome are sure to spark conversation. If you're looking for a more classic presentation, try a wrought-iron lantern or colorful watering can.

■ Croquet anyone? Challenge your neighbor to a game of miniature croquet or miniature horseshoes to take a break from your day.

■ Soften the bright green walls with pastel leather desk accessories, or create your own by using double-sided tape to affix pastel ribbon to acrylic office containers.

Faux cobblestones, beautiful flowers, and a bronze birdbath will complement your workplace garden, while a tiny watering can and a miniature game of horseshoes add function and fun.

*mod*CUBE

The mod lifestyle took hold in the early sixties as a young generation of cool cats discovered bold design and British rock. Chelsea boots, Ben Sherman apparel, and Vespa scooters infiltrated every level of society. Inseams tightened, the color wheel fell off its axle, and experimentation became de rigueur in all areas of life.

You'll put the groove back in *groovy* with a mod-inspired cube. Enhance your wall with a bold color palette and invest in an iconic Eames chair to swank up the place. Hang pictures of Twiggy and The Kinks, or a Warhol or Lichtenstein poster to add some color, then tune your CD player to Miles and Ornette or the classic "Quadrophenia." Stay as solid as Julie and Linc's *Mod Squad* as you work for the Man. Once the weekend rolls around, you'll be ready to dance in your go-go boots all night long!

Don't forget the hook for your beret!

WALLS

■ Staring at cubicle walls like those pictured on page 15 could make you dizzy, but the funky pattern transforms the space into a palace of mod. Use straight pins to hang the patterned vinyl on the lower portion of the wall. Then, to give your eyes a break, put vinyl in a color that complements the pattern up on the lower portion of the wall, pinning it along the top and sides. (For tips on working with vinyl, see page 5.)

Perpetuate the desk white-out with a white flower.

■ Cover shelves with white vinyl, affixing it with hot glue, or cover it with patterned vinyl for additional color. (For tips on working with hot glue, see page 5.)

DESK

■ Cut white vinyl to fit the top of the desk, leaving extra material so you can secure it underneath the desk with duct tape, and pull it tight .

■ Cut a 2-inch-wide (5 cm) strip of patterned vinyl and hot glue it in place along the edge of the desk to create a border.

DÉCOR

■ Select an accent color, especially if your base colors are black and white. Red is an excellent dramatic choice.

■ Use carpet circles to give the floor some color.

■ Go streamlined and modern with the lighting: Pick a lamp with a Lucite or white base and shade. For something more daring, try suspending a geometric chandelier or using a funky floor lamp.

■ Lean an oversized mod print, with colors that complement your cube, against your cubicle wall.

■ The organizer shown to the right, called a Utensilo, is perfect for the mod cube (for more information, see Resources on page 94). We've added a splash of color by popping a small vase into a compartment and filling it with bright flowers. Choose office supplies that coordinate with your mod cube.

■ Add a funky prop or two. A glass head is an ideal spot to store your sunglasses or headphones.

■ A leather padfolio, clock, or pen holder in the accent color will complement the carpet circles and mod print.

■ Fresh flowers are a great way to treat yourself and brighten your day. Include a vase by a modern designer like Jonathon Adler, with a simple orchid or a tight, all-white arrangement.

Let your colleagues know when you're in or out of the office with this paper-weight, and use a wall organizer to keep your office supplies at hand.

*glam*CUBE

Dressing for work may not require a top hat and tails, but that's no reason you can't evoke an era when tuxedos and evening gowns were worn six days a week. Fred Astaire, Ginger Rogers, Humphrey Bogart, Audrey Hepburn—each name brings to mind a more sophisticated time when boas flowed like champagne. Diamonds glittered, satin fell to the floor in sweeping majesty, swing ruled the night, and no aspiration seemed out of reach. You can soft-shoe your way to work each day as you enter your *absolutely mahvelous, dahling*, glam office space.

Fortunately, the only riches you'll need are the luxurious gold walls you'll use to design your own private Cotton Club. Listen to the music of Benny Goodman and Cole Porter to put your styling eye in the mood. Don't skimp on the silver trim as you mount life-size images of Marilyn Monroe and vintage movie posters. Strategically place a grouping of Oscars nearby as incentive to begin writing your acceptance speech—or maybe just the report your boss is waiting for. Remember, this cube calls for *much* on top of *more*. Whether faux fox or diamonds, trim to excess.

Bring back the glamorous days of a bygone era in this luxurious celebration of class and grace.

project: FRINGED DESK TRIM

MATERIALS:

- Ivory fringe, 4" long (10.2 cm)
- Rit Dye in Wine, #10
- 2 maroon feather boas
- Hot glue gun
- Hot glue

1. After covering your desk in maroon velour (as described to the right), purchase enough 4-inch-long (10.2 cm) fringe to trim the edge of your desk.

2. Following the instructions on the dye bottle, dye the fringe to match the maroon velour. Allow the fringe to dry for at least 24 hours before attaching to the desk.

3. Hang the fringe along the perimeter of the desk using a thin line of hot glue.

4. Using a hot glue gun, attach two narrow, maroon feather boas laid end to end at the top of the fringe (along the edge of the desk).

Now you can deliver that acceptance speech you've been practicing all your life.

WALLS

■ The only way to achieve ballroom elegance is with lush wallpaper. Select damask wallpaper in a champagne or gold palette. Hang the wallpaper in vertical strips, securing it to the cubicle walls with Velcro along the seams and at the top and bottom.

DESK

■ Transform your desk into an elegant vanity so you will always be ready for last-minute client dinners. Cover the surface of the desk in a deep maroon velour that will both look and feel luxurious, securing it underneath with duct tape. Finish the edge with fancy fringe and feather boas, as described in the project to the left.

DÉCOR

■ Add gold accents to your cube by displaying a replica of Oscar on your shelf—you can even have your replicas engraved with "Best Actress/Actor" and your favorite film title.

Add glitz to your cube with pearls and a fancy antique perfume bottle.

Marilyn adds glamour to any scene!

■ Select simple silver or black frames for your favorite movie posters from the 1950s, whether *Cat on a Hot Tin Roof* or *Rear Window*. This is an inexpensive way to decorate large spaces on your cubicle walls.

■ Especially when your paycheck feels small, diamonds are a girl's best friend. Place a small jewelry box on your desk and fill it with fabulous, sparkly costume jewelry. Let it spill out onto your desk, and add a pair of long gloves to enhance the "vanity" feel.

■ Let Marilyn Monroe or Clark Gable act as your own personal receptionist by placing a life-size cardboard cutout at the entry to your cube. Add a faux fur and some costume jewelry to Marilyn or a silk scarf to Clark to make them more lifelike.

■ Stack vintage luggage nearby in case you should have to jet off to Monaco. (At the very least, it might encourage you to actually use your vacation time.)

■ Add a gilded vanity mirror for last-minute touch-ups.

■ Turn your morning snack into breakfast at Tiffany's by gazing at one of the jewelry store's signature blue bags as you eat. Don't be surprised when you find your colleagues peeking inside!

*tiki*CUBE

 **T**hink your work space feels more like a dungeon of dreary then a flight of fancy? Just turn on the wave machine: The walk to your desk becomes a toe slide through the sands of your exclusive fantasy island, filled with palm trees, turquoise waters, and lots of sun. In 1934, Donn Beach, a.k.a. "Don the Beachcomber," hatched the Tiki sensation while strolling the beaches of Southern California. His idea was simple: Create an environment rich in the lush colors and motifs of Polynesian culture; add a new cocktail, the Mai-Tai; and set the music to bongo and swing. Soldiers returning from exotic locales spread the Tiki craze with souvenirs from the South Pacific.

Wrap yourself in the whimsy of Waikiki, the textures of Tahiti, or the brilliance of Bora Bora with this fun cube design. Fantasize about upcoming vacations or recall suntans past as you swirl your latte with a pink flamingo swizzle stick. Whether you construct your own private three-walled hut or set your speakers to play the sounds of ocean waves, the laid-back vibe will be unmistakable. What better way to stay relaxed when burning your torch into the wee hours?

The surf's up when you add hula skirts, Tiki accessories, and a palm tree to the mix.

Seashells and red faux coral stand out against the wood texture.

These silly Tiki mugs add a Polynesian touch.

WALLS

■ Search for fabrics or papers that will remind you of lying on a sandy beach or watching a vibrant tropical sunset. Try textured fabrics, such as burlap, or a natural-fiber wallpaper with straw running throughout. For a more affordable option, use corrugated paper printed with a tropical scene or white-capped waves, as seen above. Corrugated paper will not be long enough to cover the entire height of the wall, so you'll need to cover the wall's lower portion with solid-colored corrugated paper. Hang the paper with straight pins.

■ For a finishing touch, trim the top of the cubicle walls in bamboo. Purchase ½-inch-diameter (1.3 cm) bamboo, cut segments the length of each wall, and secure the bamboo along the upper perimeter of the corrugated paper with a hot glue gun. (For tips on working with hot glue, see page 5.) Bamboo is difficult to cut, so make sure you have a hacksaw available if it wasn't cut to fit when purchased. The bamboo will need to be held in place for 60 seconds as the glue sets.

■ Cover the flat surface of shelves with wood-grain oilcloth using hot glue and trim them with additional ½-inch-diameter (1.3 cm) bamboo.

DESK

■ To create a Tiki look that will hold up to lots of wear, cover the desk in a faux wood-grain oilcloth (as shown on page 23) or a vibrant tropical print. Cut the cloth to fit (leaving extra material to secure beneath the desk), pull the fabric tight, and secure underneath with duct tape.

■ Add a touch of whimsy by using a hot glue gun to attach table-length hula skirts around the edge of the desk.

DÉCOR

■ Incorporate elements of nature. Spray paint manzanita branches with coral red paint and place them in a corner to imitate the look of coral.

■ Nestle a fishbowl amongst the faux coral branches. To extend the color scheme, fill the fishbowl with red rocks and goldfish. Soon you will be reliving memories of scuba diving off the shores of Kailua—or dreaming of trips to come.

■ Colored glass float balls, used in years past to keep fishermen's nets afloat, add color and texture to the space.

■ Tiki mugs, hula nodders, and vintage Hawaiian prints are imperative in Polynesian pop décor. Use Tiki mugs to store office supplies or to hold your morning coffee. Several Web sites sell reproductions of Tiki paraphernalia (see Resources section on page 94).

■ A seashell with your name on it can be the perfect substitution for a nameplate.

■ Put a dashboard hula doll on the top of your computer and watch your Hawaiian beauty hula as you download your e-mail.

■ To complete the Polynesian paradise, use heavy palm matting to create the floor of your hut. Secure the mat to the floor with carpet tape so your visitors won't slip!

Tiki monsters make great pencil toppers.

Bring the aquatic life to your cube with a brightly colored fish.

*pub*CUBE

The public houses of England have been serving patrons for two thousand years, thanks to the Roman invaders who left commercial eating and drinking establishments in their wake. The best alehouses gained reputations for debauchery and rowdiness, causing the king to restrict liquor licenses in the seventh century. The mayhem continued, however, and men and women alike continued to enjoy brews and booze with their comrades.

Whether you're reveling in Ireland while watching a football match or taking it easy with your mates in Sydney, pub culture mandates welcoming all comers. Setting up your work space to reflect this attitude will invite your coworkers to substitute a break around the water cooler with an office dart tournament. Hang paper pub coasters to create collages on your walls so you can reminisce about good times out with your buddies. "Last call!" will gain new meaning when issued from within your walls!

W. C. Fields once said, "If I had to live my life over, I'd live over a saloon." Now you can work in the comfort of your own drinking hole.

Whether your game is darts . . .

. . . or pool, your cube will be full of fun and games.

WALLS ....

■ Faux wood paneling is essential to the transformation from staid cubicle to rowdy pub. Use brown-colored corrugated paper on the upper portion of the walls and faux wood corrugated paper on the lower portion. The items you hang in your pub will contrast with the brown without obscuring the texture of the faux wood paneling at the bottom. Cut the corrugated paper to fit the cubicle walls and keep it in place with strips of Velcro or straight pins on all sides.

■ Overlay shelves with dark brown felt, securing with hot glue. (For tips on working with hot glue, see page 5.) Trim the shelf with the same brown felt to keep the look clean and uncluttered.

DESK ....

■ Cover your desk with dark brown felt. Cut the fabric to fit the top of the desk (leaving extra material to secure underneath), pull the fabric tight, and secure it underneath the desk with duct tape. Use hot glue to secure any areas of fabric that pull away from the desk for a cleaner finish.

DÉCOR

■ Every pub needs a pool table, and your cube is no exception. Perch a miniature pool table, complete with cue sticks and a rack of balls, next to your phone. The next time you're on a never-ending conference call, rack 'em up!

■ Using vintage pieces in your design can evoke old-fashioned hospitality. Include a collection of vintage beer coasters or steins, or display an old wind-up bartender to serve your drink for the day.

■ Use barstools as guest chairs. If you have room, place a long shelf at table height to create a bar in your cube.

■ Collect a variety of bar towels and hang them as art, or place them on a shelf—they'll come in handy for cleaning up coffee spills!

■ Neon beer signs are a decorating must for any bar, and they also provide lighting that sets the proper mood. Call your favorite local beer distributor to see if they have any for sale.

■ Scour eBay and other Web sites for vintage posters advertising your favorite beer or an old Irish pub, frame them, and hang them on the wall.

■ Wooden containers can hold your office supplies, and are compatible with the pub look.

■ Put a small refrigerator in your cube to keep cold beverages on hand. Even if you can't have a beer at the end of the day, iced tea or a gourmet soda pop will refresh you.

■ Don't forget a bowl of bar snacks. Peanuts, pretzels, or chips are a perfect midday munch.

■ Turn a galvanized metal bucket with your favorite beer logo into a trash can.

■ Use a beer coolie to store your pens and pencils, and a beer tap as a paperweight.

Your own personal bartender!

*nap*CUBE

Studies clearly indicate that people are more sleep-deprived than ever before. When not at work, we're running errands, socializing, and exercising. The truth is, we could all use a nap. Did you know JFK and Winston Churchill both curled up most afternoons? Even Napoleon Bonaparte and Thomas Edison made time in their busy lives for a midday slumber. Well-rested people are more productive at work, but naptime conflicts with the demands of the modern world.

Curling up in your cube may seem like a crazy notion, but what if there were fuzzy slippers on your feet and a cozy throw spread across your lap? You could discover comfort nirvana in an otherwise hectic day. Midnight blue walls covered with stars invite rest, and after the yawns subside, you'll revel in your role as the most lucid thinker in the room. Perhaps even the executives will add a resting cot to their corner offices once they witness the transformative power of a nap.

They say a 15-minute nap will invigorate and refresh. Just make' sure you take it in style!

A cereal dispenser makes a post-nap snack neat and easy.

Trim the top perimeter of the wall with cotton batting, attaching it with hot glue, but take care not to burn your hand, as the glue could seep through the batting. (For tips on working with hot glue, see page 5.) Pluck the surface of the batting to create a cloudlike look.

Cover shelves with silver vinyl, securing the vinyl to the surface with hot glue. (For tips on working with vinyl, see page 5.) Then, trim the edges with the fluffy cotton batting.

DESK

Cover the top surface of the desk with silver vinyl. Cut the vinyl to fit (leaving extra material to secure underneath), pull tight, and secure it underneath the desk with duct tape. If there are areas of vinyl that pull away from the desk around the perimeter, secure it with double-sided tape or hot glue for a clean finish.

Using flat-head tacks, secure a length of white tulle to the perimeter of the desk to create a sleep curtain that will dim the bright lights of your office. Add a second layer of tulle for a fuller curtain.

To trim the perimeter of the desk, place a strip of cotton batting over the flat-head tacks and secure with hot glue.

WALLS

Glitter, glitter, and more glitter! The walls shown on page 31 are very simple to create and are all about the adornment. Cut midnight blue corrugated paper to fit the walls and secure them with Velcro or straight pins around the edges. Hang silver glitter stars randomly all over the available wall space to create a starry sky.

DÉCOR

No nap space is complete without a comfy bed. Purchase a foam mattress 6 inches (15 cm) thick and cut it with scissors to fit the space underneath your desk. Add some flannel sheets, a comfy blanket, and a pillow or two, and you have the perfect spot for a 15-minute catnap.

Cereal is a good meal at any time of the day, but even better when you eat it with flair. Purchase a cereal dispenser, and with a turn of your wrist your favorite cereal comes tumbling out. Keep a ceramic milk carton on hand for decoration—it can stay in your

Don't miss that meeting!

A soft night-light adds to the ambiance of your nap cube.

cube forever, minus the milk, without having to be tossed.

■ A cluster of charming vintage alarm clocks ensures you don't miss that important meeting after your nap.

■ A night-light adds a soft glow, mellowing the fluorescent lighting that most cube-dwellers endure every day.

■ In addition to your trade magazines, policies, and manuals, keep some of your favorite books and magazines on hand for pre-slumber reads.

■ Invite guests to join your slumber.

They can snuggle in an oversized chair with lush pillows and a throw, and make themselves at home.

■ Keep a pair of comfortable slippers, an eye mask, and ear plugs nearby to put you in a tranquil state of mind.

■ Create your own relaxing lavender spray with a small atomizer, distilled water, and lavender essential oil. Fill the atomizer with water and add five drops of essential oil to create a soothing aroma in your cube.

■ Tune in to your favorite classical radio station to alleviate your stress with calming music.

*india*CUBE

Imagine India and you conjure up saffron and magenta hues and cumin and curry aromas. Whether you're harking back to the earliest Indus Valley civilizations or the pageantry of Bollywood, you'll discover that India offers an array of style options that combines traditionalism, mystical novelty, and discriminating aesthetics.

India is one of the world's greatest cultural centers. This second most populated country hosts every major religion and artfully mixes tradition with its modern, contemporary culture. A space designed in Indo-fashion can include an image of the Hindu god Ganesh and a poster of film star Akshay Kumar. A statue of Siddhartha, the great Buddha, will bring good luck to any business meeting. Creating a background of deep reds and saffron will allay visual distraction and allow calm to settle over you. Fuse the traditional and the contemporary to create a visual mosaic of paisley and pop, celebrating the majesty of the Indian subcontinent!

The mysticism and bright colors of India will add beauty and style to your cube.

WALLS

◼ Saris come in a variety of prints and bold colors and can provide a dramatic wall covering. Measure your walls first to ensure you purchase enough material, and select your favorite saris at a store that carries international goods. Fasten each sari to the top of the walls with straight pins, gather the fabric in the middle of the wall (see page 35), and pin each end of the gathered section to create a swag.

◼ Using hot glue, line the top of the wall with a simple strand of red plastic disks or beads that complements your sari. (For tips on working with hot glue, see page 5.)

◼ Cover the surface of the shelf in gold lamé or vinyl and trim the edges with strands of coordinating plastic disks or beads. Attach both covering and trim with hot glue. (For tips on working with vinyl, see page 5.)

DESK

◼ This cube is all about jewel tones, with accents in gold. Cover the desk in gold lamé or vinyl, securing it with duct tape underneath the desk. Trim the edges of the desk with coordinating disks or beads affixed to the vinyl with hot glue.

DÉCOR

◼ Brass accessories add warmth and sparkle. Display a brass vase, frame your favorite photograph in brass, or put pencils and pens in a brass cup.

◼ Carved wood bookends and decorative iron pots provide visual stimulation and contrasting textures.

Your French press and a set of glasses will serve you well when you take a break with colleagues, while candles and fine, antique accessories accent the gold tones.

◼ Colorful perfume bottles in a variety of sizes will add a sense of romance to your design.

◼ A wooden organizer accented with hammered metal is the perfect container for office supplies.

◼ A lamp with a colorful beaded shade casts an appealing glow while playing off the trim of the walls and desk.

◼ Line the cubicle with 3- or 4-foot-tall (91 or 122 cm) iron candlesticks topped with colorful votive candleholders to add a homey feeling and a warm candle-lit glow.

◼ Give your cubicle depth by placing a dark-colored bench in front of the iron candlesticks.

◼ Hang a painting of an Indian icon that coordinates with the jewel-toned saris.

◼ Brew fresh Darjeeling tea in a French press, and keep bright Mediterranean tea glasses on hand for serving.

◼ Colorful fruit in a wood or brass platter is not only a healthy afternoon snack, but also adds to the depth of color in your cube.

*golf*CUBE

Every golfer knows the daydreams: the shot you wish had been a mulligan on the last round, or the hole you wish you'd used your pitching wedge for rather than your 9-iron. Golf draws in even the casual player with equal parts exhilaration and frustration. So why not look up from your work and escape to St. Andrews Road Hole or the 18th at Pebble Beach? Hang your favorite dogleg above your monitor and let the strategizing begin! A little Astroturf and some silver trophies will go a long way toward replicating Augusta on your bookshelf.

The possibilities surrounding the golf cube are as endless as a 600-yard par 5. Just adding some of your favorite golf tomes from Nicklaus or Hogan, with their classic green spines, gives character to your layout. An antique bag with an old set of clubs and a screensaver of your favorite holes will serve as a reminder that you'd rather be driving, pitching, and putting. Your work space will double as the 19th hole for your entire office, a verdant fantasy to take a stroke off the clock—and perhaps off your scorecard.

Be sure to practice your putting before you head out to the green!

project: DESKTOP BUNKER

MATERIALS:

- Cardboard
- Chicken wire
- Hot glue gun
- Hot glue
- Astroturf
- Green felt
- Natural-colored decorative sand

1. Cut a piece of cardboard to fit the corner of your desk, approximately 24 inches long by 17 inches wide (61 cm by 43 cm).

2. Form the chicken wire into a shallow bowl and carefully hot glue the bottom of the chicken wire to the cardboard. Take care to protect your fingers from the wire after it's been heated by the hot glue.

3. Cover the chicken wire in Astroturf and cut the Astroturf to fit. Attach the Astroturf to the chicken wire using hot glue, and hold the Astroturf against the chicken wire as the glue sets.

4. Trim the perimeter of the cardboard in 1-inch-wide (2.5 cm) green felt to cover the seam between the desk and the bunker you've created.

5. Use hot glue to secure the bunker to the corner of your desk.

6. Fill the bunker with natural-colored decorative sand, and stick your pens and pencils in.

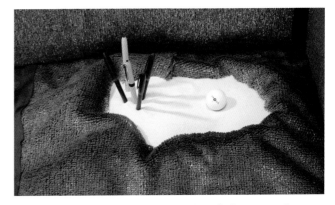

Your desktop bunker will be the most unique desk accessory in the office!

WALLS

■ Wall-to-wall Astroturf creates the backdrop for your hole in one. Astroturf is fairly heavy, so you'll need to apply two strips of Velcro around the edges of the cubicle walls to keep it hanging. Use straight pins for extra security.

■ Cover the flat surface of the shelves with Astroturf and apply 2-inch-wide (5 cm) strips of green felt to the edges with hot glue. Be sure to cover the edges of the Astroturf with the felt, as they are likely to fray. (For tips on working with hot glue, see page 5.)

DESK

■ Cut Astroturf to fit your desktop, leaving extra material to secure underneath, and stick it to the surface with hot glue.

■ Line the desk with a 2- to 3-inch-wide (5 to 7.6 cm) strip of green felt to complete the look and cover up any fraying edges. Hot glue the felt to the top and bottom of the desk.

DÉCOR

■ Store your golf clubs and shoes nearby. They just might inspire an early afternoon golf game!

Display a golf trophy to show off your skills on the green.

■ Pin up articles listing tips to improve your golf game or information on your favorite courses.

■ Scour antique stores for golf memorabilia—vintage golf trophies can double as office storage when you fill them with rubber bands or paper clips.

■ With 2-inch-diameter (5 cm) plumbing pipe, create a flag for your 19th hole. Cover the pipe with white duct tape, then cut red vinyl into a triangular flag. Secure the flag to the top of the pole with double-sided tape. Fore!

■ Clear cylinder containers filled with golf balls and tees remind you that your next game's only a few hours away.

■ A leather golf bag makes a great trash can and lends an authentic touch.

A vintage bank is a perfect accessory for your cube, and keeping golf balls and tees on hand will ensure you're always prepared for a game.

■ Can't wait to get on the golf course? Gather your coworkers in your cube for some action on the putting green with a practice cup. It's the best way to relieve stress, and it will get your mind off those pesky reports you have to do!

*nyc*CUBE

Close your eyes and conjure up the sound of honking horns, the smell of pretzels, and the energy of a rush of people flowing past you at breakneck speed, and you've got the quintessential American city—New York, New York. From Lower Manhattan to Yankee Stadium, the Big Apple provides all things urban to people from all walks of life: fine dining, fabulous shopping, and an edgy attitude. To both tourists seeing a show on Broadway and natives riding the subway to work, New York City infuses the soul with an unmistakable energy.

Create your own mini metropolis with taxicab-yellow tones and an array of model cabs on your shelves and desk. Whether you're thinking Broadway or the Bowery, Midtown or Downtown, images of the city will take you and your coworkers on an instant trip.

Bright city lights, red apples, and yellow taxicabs bring the New York way of life to your cube.

WALLS

■ Set the scene with a large poster of the Manhattan skyline at night. Many online resources offer such posters. Hang with straight pins or Velcro. Don't worry if the poster doesn't cover the entire wall—just add a horizontal piece of black corrugated paper or vinyl to fill in the rest.

■ Line shelves with black vinyl held in place with hot glue, and use black duct tape to cover the edges. (For tips on working with vinyl and hot glue, see page 5.)

DESK

■ Create your own version of a New York checkered cab by lining your desk with taxicab-yellow vinyl. Cut the vinyl to fit the surface of the desk (leaving extra material to secure underneath), pull tight, and secure vinyl with duct tape underneath the desk.

■ Trim the desk with a 2-inch-wide (5 cm) black-and-white checkered ribbon to finish off your taxi.

DÉCOR

■ A large map of the New York subway system or city streets is a good way to adorn your walls and may inspire you to hit the streets.

Show you love New York with a King Kong figurine, a classic mug, checkerboard taxi models, and a clock constructed out of a taxicab medallion.

■ Touristy King Kong and Empire State Building salt and pepper shakers are not just great decoration, they'll make eating lunch at your desk more fun, too.

■ Place a stack of New York travel guides and historical books on your shelf for visitors and colleagues to peruse, and flank them with Brooklyn Bridge or other New York–themed bookends.

■ Whether you're a Yankees or Mets fan, fill your cube with memorabilia to invoke team spirit. Place a jersey on the back of your chair, hang your favorite baseball hat on the wall, or frame an old black-and-white photograph of one of New York's historic stadiums, like Ebbets Field.

■ Time flies in the city, but there's no better way to count the minutes until 5:00 than on a clock made out of a New York taxicab shield.

■ Keep a bowl of red apples on your desk, and offer them to your coworkers for a healthy afternoon snack.

■ Include a director's chair for your guests to relax in as homage to the famous Broadway shows, and sip your morning coffee from an "I ♥ New York" mug.

■ Place a miniature replica of the Statue of Liberty on your desk as a reminder that freedom is only hours away!

*cabin*CUBE

Backpacking gives you the opportunity to disappear for a spell into idyllic meadows or verdant forests. When you're enveloped by trees, camping beneath a starry night sky, the world becomes simpler. Surrounding yourself with reminders of natural settings won't replace your time in the great outdoors, but it will help remind you that there's more to life than cities, commutes, and commerce.

Lean back in your chair and follow the trail away from the day's hassles and into a rustic cabin nestled in the woods. Gather arboreal reminders from trips gone by to gain inspiration for treks to come. Post a map or two of your favorite hiking regions, and you'll be able to escape into your own magical world. Adding a lantern for light and a comfortable chair with a fleece throw will ensure you have a place to sit back and reflect. And who needs a campfire when you can have a s'more maker? You may only be camped out in front of your computer screen, but at least you can leave the mosquito spray in your briefcase.

Escape to the great outdoors and keep your hiking boots on hand for a ramble in the woods with your colleagues.

A comfortable wicker chair will be a warm welcome to colleagues.

WALLS

■ Focus on creating a cozy environment by using camel, chocolate, green, and red tones to layer the colors of fall onto your walls. Corrugated paper printed with beautifully colored autumn leaves is a good choice. Secure the corrugated paper to the walls with straight pins.

■ Gather fallen branches and bundle them with string to frame your cubicle walls. Secure the bundles to the cube with a small circle of hot glue. (For tips on working with hot glue, see page 5.) No time to gather twigs? Visit your local display and costume store and search for faux birch branches, like those shown on page 47. Gluing a thick band of the branches in a horizontal line along the middle of the wall will create a chair rail to add depth and a cabinlike feel to your space.

■ Cover shelves with camel-colored felt. Cut the felt to cover the flat surface of the shelf, and secure with hot glue. Add a 2-inch-wide (5 cm) suede ribbon with chocolate brown suede stitching to create a border for the shelf, and glue in place.

DESK

■ Cover the desk in camel-colored felt or a fabric that reminds you of your favorite rugged shirt, whether flannel, fleece, or denim. Cut the fabric to fit the top of the desk (leaving extra material to secure underneath with duct tape) and pull tight. If there are areas of the fabric that pull away from the desk around the perimeter, secure with hot glue for a cleaner finish.

■ Finish by trimming the desk to match the style of the shelves, using a 2-inch-wide (5 cm) suede ribbon that coordinates with your fabric.

Candlelight and real wooden pencils complement the faux birch trim.

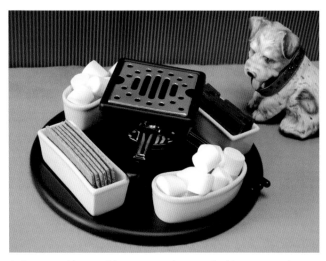

A s'more machine provides an excuse for a snack with your coworkers.

DÉCOR

■ Bringing the outdoors indoors is the key to evoking a rustic ambiance. Gather pinecones, stones, and branches, and place them in eye-catching places around the cubicle.

■ Faux pine trees add depth, and placing a group of three near the entrance to your cubicle will instantly create the atmosphere of a family cabin in the mountains.

■ A wicker chair with a down-filled cushion will encourage your coworkers to stay awhile. Wicker comes in several colors and tones; to create a warm environment, a deeper tone is best.

■ Rummage through your closet and bring your hiking attire and gear to work. A worn pair of hiking boots, a fur hat, or a walking stick can initiate conversations about the hike you took in Yosemite.

■ Woodcarvings placed in a corner or on a shelf add height and dimension to your cabin cube. Search for rustic knick-knacks at your favorite antique store, or pick up a carving at a roadside stop on your next mountain adventure.

■ A large painting of mountain scenery in a rustic log frame makes a great focal point. If you don't have a painting, look through your photographs to find a favorite autumn scene to enlarge and frame.

■ Keep a battery-operated lantern ready for additional desk lighting. (You'll also be prepared for any power outage.)

■ Colored pencils with carved wood handles are a fun and useful accessory on your desk. Create your own rustic containers by hot gluing small twigs around a cup to hold your pencils and pens.

collector's CUBE

 Collecting is no longer a pastime enjoyed only by the retired and the eccentric. Whether you covet seashells or alarm clocks, Fabergé eggs or Japanese animé figurines, collecting is a hobby that combines history and the thrill of discovery. Best of all, this activity requires only as little or as much attention as you're willing to commit and is feasible within any budget.

Displaying your collectibles at work creates a visually exciting work space as well as an instant conversation starter. Once you arrange your collection of choice, you can accent walls with posters from collector conferences or photographs of the elusive item that you simply must have. Unique, colorful containers and a funky lamp contribute to the kitschy feel. Once you start decorating, you'll discover that your special collection of meaningful mementos will brighten even the dullest day!

Nothing screams fun and kitsch like bright colors and fun collectibles.

WALLS

■ Contemporary collecting is often about kitsch, so play it up! The color palette can range from baby blue or pink to bright red or kiwi green. Prevent color overload by dividing the wall into two sections. First, hang a panel of white vinyl on the top portion of the wall and secure around the edges with straight pins. (For tips on working with vinyl, see page 5.) Add color by pinning a panel textured with bright pom-pom fringe on the lower portion of the wall, as in the photo on page 51. Ensure that the white isn't too sharp a contrast by covering the top portion of the wall with a piece of pale-colored tulle held in place with straight pins.

■ Trim the top perimeter of the wall with a paper fringe, securing it to the vinyl with hot glue. (For tips on working with hot glue, see page 5.)

■ Cover shelves with kitschy pink vinyl with white polka dots (or plain white vinyl), and trim using hot glue with white paper fringe or pom-pom fringe in the same bright color as the lower portion of the wall.

DESK

■ Combine a retro color palette with fun, interesting shapes to add depth. Find a patterned material, and cut it to fit the desk with some excess so you can secure it underneath the desk with duct tape. Create a half-skirt around the desk with the textured vinyl you used on the lower portion of the wall, then hot glue pom-pom fringe to the perimeter of your desk.

DÉCOR

■ Your favorite collection, whether antique dishes, comic books, or bobbleheads, will perk up a bad day. Display on your desk and shelves.

■ Serve bubble gum and retro candies in a group of clear glass cylinders in various shapes and sizes. A clock with oversized numbers will ensure you don't miss the end of your workday!

■ A lamp with a mercury glass base (you can purchase one at a home goods store) is an inexpensive item that adds both a vintage feel and a modern shape to your collection. Paint the inside of a white lampshade with your chosen color for a dazzling addition to your desk.

■ Whimsical containers intended to hold cotton balls and cotton swabs are easily transformed into unique storage bins for paper clips, rubber bands, and pushpins. Consider using a brightly colored toothbrush holder for pen and pencil storage.

■ When done in moderation, layering materials can give your cube depth, and you can personalize your space by creating vignettes or patterns. Layer circular rugs on a rectangular rug to cover ugly industrial carpet and add dimension to your work space.

Quirky figurines, colorful candies, and kitschy office supply containers will make your work space pop with personality.

C.E.O.CUBE

 Everyone's heard stories about those CEOs who began their ascent to the executive suite from the basement mailroom. You might not occupy the corner office at the top of the building yet, but there's no reason you should appoint your work space with any less style. Trump's digs might be more expansive, Gates's may be loftier, but set your sights on their positions of power and decorate your cube as though you've already made it to the top.

Nothing says success like a corner office with a view. Give yourself a faux window with a downtown view of the New York, London, or Hong Kong skyline. Accessorize your desk with a chrome-colored mouse and black leather desk pad, pen holder, and paper trays to lay your claim to today's CEO excess. Upgrade your chair to the executive level and you'll be running the company in no time.

Climbing the corporate ladder will be easy once you have an office worthy of an executive.

project: CREATING A VIEW

MATERIALS:
- Cardboard
- Box cutter
- Spray adhesive
- 3' x 2.5' (91 cm x 76.2 cm) poster of city view
- Small hacksaw
- 1"-wide (2.5 cm) unpainted crown molding
- Hot glue gun
- Hot glue
- Ivory-colored spray paint

1. Use a box cutter to cut cardboard to the size of the poster.

2. Spray the cardboard with the adhesive and mount the back of poster to the cardboard to create a durable backing.

3. Use a hacksaw to cut the crown molding to fit the perimeter of the poster, creating a frame. Cut the ends of the molding on a diagonal and secure together with hot glue to create corners.

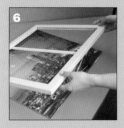

4. Cut another section of crown molding to fit vertically across the middle of the poster, creating a window effect.

5. Spray the crown molding with ivory paint and let it dry overnight.

6. Line the back of the frame with hot glue, and place it on top of the poster, creating a framed window.

7. Hang your window on a cubicle wall within your line of sight so you can gaze out at your view.

WALLS

- Cover the walls in a rich merlot velour fabric, secured with Velcro around the edges, to introduce a sense of opulence and luxury.
- For an elegant, finished façade, trim the top and bottom of the walls in a cream crown molding, available at hardware stores. Have molding precut to the size of your cubicle walls so it fits together correctly. Hold the molding in place with Velcro.

DESK

- Executive offices are designed to aid productivity, so clear the clutter and create a space with clean lines, steel, and black leather. If you can't swing a vintage metal desk from the company supply room, cover the surface of your desk in steel-gray velour.
- Trim the desk with a 2-inch-wide (5 cm) strip of gray velour to create a clean, monotone look. Wrap the velour strip around the edge of the desk and secure to the top and bottom of the desk with a thin line of hot glue. (For tips on using hot glue, see page 5.)

DÉCOR

- Bringing a bookcase into your cube adds dimension as well as storage space. Leather-bound books, metal accessories, model cars, and chrome bookends create sleek lines while suggesting that you enjoy the finer things in life.
- You've worked hard to earn that diploma! Make sure you take the time to frame it appropriately and find the ideal spot in your cubicle to keep your credentials on display.
- When purchasing office supplies, remember to consider their color and design—think more Mont Blanc and less Bic. A steel-gray paper shredder is a must to protect yourself from

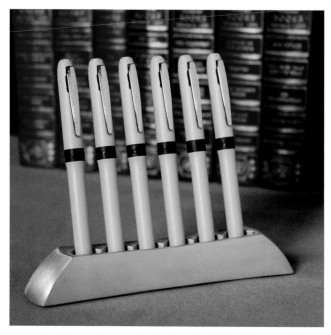

Keep plenty of pens on hand to sign those big contracts.

corporate espionage, and black leather boxes and chrome accessories say "movin' on up" like nothing else.

■ Offering your guests an espresso from your silver or black espresso machine will impress even the most difficult of your clients. Then let them recline in a modern black-and-chrome side chair and indulge in your opulence.

■ Replace your standard desk chair with an ergonomic chair that offers support and comfort as you burn the candle at both ends.

■ Use black-and-white photographs of your friends and family to accent the black leather accessories on your desk. The photographs will pop on the backdrop of the merlot-colored walls.

Power accessories, like a model Mercedes-Benz, silver serving pieces, and business magazines, will ensure you move up in the corporate world.

*casino*CUBE

There's no place quite like Vegas—except maybe Monte Carlo. Casino towns have evolved beyond just slot machines and kitschy entertainment to pack more excitement into a weekend than you usually experience in six months. The mystique of money quickly gained (and lost!) combines with glamour and the captivation of onlookers to create an ambience dripping with decadence. You may want to schedule a "research retreat" to Sin City to bolster your design (and your design budget).

The clashing of color and texture should dominate in the casino cubicle. Cover your walls with a roulette wheel and a deck of cards to give the space an authentic feel of having been there. Green felt and a little neon go a long way toward transforming your boring work space into a glitzy palace. Well-placed chips and dice add to the ambience while providing a quick break activity for coworkers. Craps, anyone?

Gold, glitz, and green felt bring the luck of the draw straight to your office space.

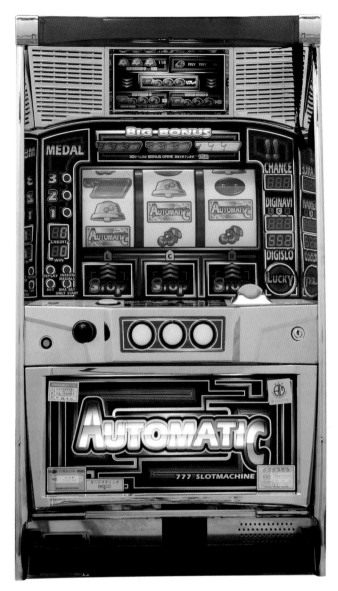

Your personal slot machine will provide fun for late nights at the office, and you might even win big!

WALLS

■ Use your cubicle walls as a landscape for your own gaming room. Cover the walls in green felt, securing the felt with Velcro strips along the edges. You could also purchase a package of felt that is printed to mimic a blackjack or craps table. Trim the printed felt into sections, creating several different gaming areas.

■ Line shelves in green felt as well by cutting felt to size and hot gluing it to the surfaces. (For tips on using hot glue, see page 5.) Finish off with a strip of green felt to trim the edge of the shelves. Secure the trim with hot glue.

DESK

■ Nothing says "casino" like gold. Cover the desk in gold-colored vinyl, securing it underneath with duct tape to create the perfect contrast to the green walls. (For tips on working with vinyl, see page 5.)

■ Trim the desk in a gold fringe table skirt hot glued to the gold vinyl. For some extra glitter, glue to the top of the fringe a 2-inch-wide (5 cm) strip of gold sequins around the edge of the desk.

DÉCOR

■ Use spray paint to take something old and make it new again. A white column or pedestal from a flea market or an antique store is easily transformed by spraying it with gold paint. Add some glitz to your desk lamp by spraying the shade and base gold.

■ Fill a clear glass container with chocolate coins in gold wrappers. Spill some out onto the desk to share with your guests.

■ Highlight your cubicle with a large slot machine positioned in a corner with the handle ready to pull. Have a supply of tokens available so coworkers can play, and keep inexpensive prizes

Welcome to Las Vegas—what happens in your cube, stays in your cube.

Dress up a mannequin to add mystery and flair.

on hand to give out if someone hits the jackpot.

■ Neon is imperative for creating the sparkle of the Vegas Strip. Place neon signs on corners, shelves, and even the top of the slot machine.

■ Games provide the perfect diversion during a long lunch break or at the end of a long afternoon. Your luck could change with the spin of a miniature bingo cage or a roulette wheel, and you could win big!

■ Frame your desk chair and office binders with 2-inch-wide (5 cm) strips of gold sequins to add sparkle.

■ Visit your local costume store and pick up a mix of masks adorned in feathers. Nestle a mask among your books or place it on a nearby shelf to recall the pageantry of Vegas showgirls.

■ Stacks of poker chips and cards are a must. Use hot glue to secure a stack of chips, a hand of cards, a plastic glass, and a cocktail napkin on the walls to create a 3-D vignette.

■ Hang metallic dollar signs and spinning strands of metallic paper throughout the space for added dimension.

*rock*CUBE

Music has influenced other art forms throughout history, but no genre has had as much impact on the cultural landscape as rock 'n' roll. Jim Morrison's and Janis Joplin's attitudes and personal styles changed our hemlines, language, and culture. And today, rockin' out is easier than ever: Create your own Fillmore East in your office cube with vintage rock posters, LP jackets, and Rolling Stones album covers. Your rock star ensemble is certain to give your colleagues flashbacks (even if they can't remember all the details).

Whether you go old school with a black light and velvet or keep it contemporary with a poster from last week's gig, the rock cube will leave you cranking up your desktop speakers as you dive into the wall of sound.

Playing tunes and perusing *Rolling Stone* during your break will ensure your day flies by.

Old concert T-shirts showcase your road-warrior past.

WALLS

■ Recreate your wild days with red vinyl walls. Cut the vinyl to fit the walls and attach with straight pins around the edges. (For tips on working with vinyl, see page 5.) Then tack red tie-dyed mesh at the top and bottom of the cubicle walls to add layers, and tear a few holes so the red vinyl peeks through. Apply a strip of red duct tape along the top and bottom perimeter to cover the flat heads of the tacks.

Even if you can't play a lick, a Fender will make your cube rock-ready.

■ Cover shelves with red vinyl, using hot glue, and trim the edges of the shelves with ribbon adorned with flames. (For tips on working with hot glue, see page 5.)

DESK

■ Wild animal prints will put you in touch with your inner rock 'n' roll animal, so break out some zebra-print upholstery fabric to cover your desk. Cut the fabric to fit the desk, leaving extra material to secure underneath with duct tape, and pull tight. If there are areas of the fabric that pull away from the desk around the edge, secure it with double-sided tape for a clean finish.

DÉCOR

■ Exploring music stores can take hours, but finding a vintage Jimi Hendrix album cover to adorn your cubical wall makes it well worth the effort.

■ Show your roots with a tour poster of your favorite hair band.

■ Trim a bulletin board with flaming ribbon, or paint the frame with metallic paint. Add concert tickets from memorable shows or a postcard promoting one you want to attend.

■ Post sheet music of popular rock songs on your wall; it might be just the inspiration you need to learn to play the guitar.

■ Lay out a mouse pad featuring your favorite band or, as shown here, the famous tongue from the Rolling Stones.

■ Place a used electric guitar in a corner on a stand, even if you don't play.

■ Build a rack to hang a collection of your worn-in concert T-shirts. String medium-gauge wire underneath the shelf, and hang your T-shirts from the wire on hangers.

■ Create a gold record of your very own by covering a vinyl in gold spray paint. Let the paint dry for 24 hours, and create a label on your computer for the center. Affix the label with

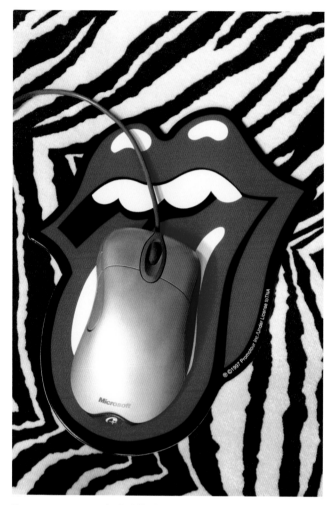

Even your mouse can be funkified!

spray adhesive and mount the album (with a listing of the name, release date, and record company beneath it) on cardboard using hot glue. Frame the mounted record in a simple black frame, and hang on your wall.

*sci-fi***CUBE**

For anyone who might feel like an alien in the office from time to time, there's no better way to customize your cube than with a space pod worthy of George Lucas. Why not teleport yourself to the captain's seat of your own enterprise in an intergalatic cube of the future?

All great science begins with scribbled equations, and your work pod will show evidence of your genius. Include cryptic messages and riddles within the polynomials to engage your colleagues' consciousness, and perhaps they will return the favor by scrawling an equation or two for you to solve when you reenter orbit from a long afternoon meeting. Add a few of your favorite sci-fi movie posters from an earlier era to fill the black holes. A toy robot, complete with moving limbs and blinking lights, proves a futuristic desktop invention. Display meteorite specimens, add a dash of moon soil, and your cube is ready for liftoff!

Create a mix of *The Twilight Zone* and *The X-Files* for a cube that is truly out there.

WALLS

■ Your cubical can be one giant blackboard with walls made of chalk cloth. Cut panels of cloth to fit each cubicle wall; due to the weight of the heavy material, hang it with a double strip of Velcro around the edges. If you're having a difficult time securing the cloth, use black duct tape for extra staying power.

■ Cut black vinyl to fit shelves and use hot glue to attach. (For tips on working with vinyl and hot glue, see page 5.)

DESK

■ Purchase silver or purple vinyl to cover your desk. Cut the vinyl to fit the top of the desk, pull tight, and use duct tape to secure the vinyl underneath the desk. If there are areas of the fabric that pull away from the desk around the perimeter, secure them with double-sided tape for a clean finish.

■ Trim the desk with a 2-inch-wide (5 cm) band of black metallic mesh, and hold in place with black flat-head tacks.

DÉCOR

■ Creative lighting is easily achieved with the jumbo-sized lightbulb lamp shown on the shelf on page 67 (for more information, see Resources on page 95).

■ Your guests will feel as though they're about to blast into outer space when they sit in a chair that lights up!

■ What science fiction cube would be complete without aliens? Paint a foam mannequin head green and put a

An extraterrestrial in your cube proves that the truth is out there.

An alien rock paperweight, a funky robot clock, and smart mathematical formulas are perfect for this cube.

plastic alien costume mask on it. If an invasion is called for, create several aliens, and group them together. If you're more a fan of sci-fi horror, cover a foam mannequin with a Frankenstein mask instead.

■ Hang retro posters for sci-fi movies like *The Forbidden Planet* or *Close Encounters of the Third Kind*.

■ All mad scientists have creative ways of tracking time, so look for a clock in the shape of a robot or spaceship.

■ Make sure you have stacks of geometry, chemistry, and science fiction books for inspiration.

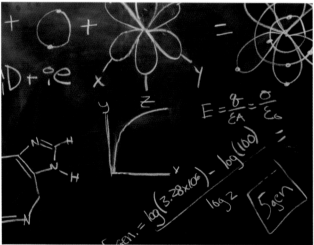

*hip-hop*CUBE

In 1976, Kool Herc exported Jamaica's fresh, trademark sound of cut-and-mixed records to the streets of the South Bronx. Grandmaster Flash soon followed suit by perfecting the scratch, and went live in '79 with his streets-inspired turntable skills. Over the next 25-plus years, the raw urban tone and flashy style of hip-hop and rap have revolutionized pop culture again and again, from Run DMC to Tupac, from Jay-Z to OutKast.

Paying homage to your favorite hip-hop idols will be a key element in defining your cube, while graffiti and bling will transform your cube into an urban paradise. Pick a coast and get kickin': East Coast? Use brick elements and a touch of ice to evoke the streets of New York. West Coast? Trick out your desk and chair with glow lights, find a pair of LA-style palm trees, and install some slammin' rims. Officemates will be looking for the velvet ropes so they can line up and check you out!

Pimping out your work space will keep it real when you have to keep it at work.

project: CONCRETE WALLS

MATERIALS:

- Medium-strength card-board large enough to cover cubicle walls
- 2 cans of gray spray paint
- 4 cans of gray faux stone spray paint
- Colored spray paint

1. Cut the cardboard to fit the cubicle walls, marking which panel goes along which wall. (This will be important when you tag them!)

2. Spray one coat of gray paint onto the cardboard to provide a good base for the faux stone. Let the cardboard dry for at least 24 hours.

3. Spray each painted cardboard panel with the faux stone spray paint, holding the can at least 12 inches (30 cm) from the surface. There will be small specs of white and black in the spray paint, which will create the appearance of concrete. Apply at least two coats for a realistic look, and allow the spray paint to dry for another 24 hours.

4. To mark this cube as your own, you'll want to display your tag in bright, vibrant colors. Dig through old hip-hip album covers at your local record shop, then sketch out your design and use colored spray paint to create your signature tag. Follow the directions on the right to hang your concrete wall.

WALLS

- Hang faux concrete walls (see project, at left) with C-clamps, which will provide a rough, unfinished look that is perfect for this urban cube. The walls can also be hung with strips of Velcro.
- Using hot glue, cover shelves in gray vinyl and trim with gray industrial piping. (For tips on working with vinyl and hot glue, see page 5.)

DESK

- Cover your desk in gray felt to create the feel of concrete. Cut the fabric to fit the top of the desk (leaving extra material to secure underneath), pull tight, and secure underneath the desk with duct tape.
- Add a strand of clear rope lights to the edge of your desk by securing them with Velcro. Pay attention to where your outlets are and orient the lights so the plug is near the outlet. Frame the lights on the top and bottom with ¼-inch-wide (6.4 cm) dark gray foam trim. The foam will need to be hot glued to the felt trim underneath and held in place as it sets (about 30 seconds).

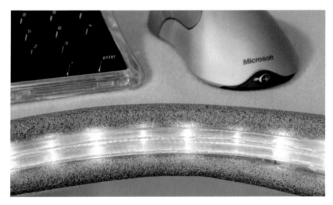

A strand of lights adds extra flash.

Urbanize your cube with blazin' graffiti.

Have plenty of ice on hand to show coworkers your playa style.

DÉCOR

■ There's nothing like a spinner to encapsulate the full pimped-out effect. Spinning rims can cost upward of $2,500, so finding an affordable alternative takes some digging. Visit your local costume shop first, and if you're unable to find a faux rim, pay a visit to your local junkyard.

■ Stack piles of books on the history of hip-hop on your shelves and see how many of your colleagues remember the Adidas shell toes or all the words to "Rapper's Delight" and "Fight For Your Right to Party."

■ Spread a gray shag rug on the floor to evoke pavement and concrete.

■ Faux diamond necklaces, rings, and medallions will mark your office as a playa's cube. Or add a cup pimped out in bling for lattes on late evenings.

■ Don't forget a classic boombox with your favorite hip-hop tunes for long Friday afternoons when everyone's ready to relax.

■ Post articles and advertisements from *Vibe* and *The Source* on a magnetic board for extra flava.

■ Hang fuzzy dice from one of your shelves and put a basketball in the corner of your cubicle.

■ Complete the urban look with metal office supply holders and containers. Hot glue faux diamonds to them so you can show off your ice.

cubism CUBE

During the early 1900s, Pablo Picasso and Georges Braque inspired each other to transform their appreciation of African sculpture and the art of Cézanne and Seurat into a controversial new school of art. Although their work was criticized as nothing more than "schemes and cubes" by a prominent Parisian art critic, the two persevered to create cubism. Artists of this movement denounced perspective by emphasizing every feature of an image equally; they revolutionized visual art and established modern art's legitimacy.

Creating your own cubist masterpiece will have coworkers coming by for gallery tours, and you can keep your artwork fresh by adding new discoveries every week. Tack up shards of a musical score juxtaposed with pages of your favorite prose, or define yourself in an evolving collage. Drop some of Matisse's bold colors or Cézanne's post-Impressionism onto your canvas. You'll be deemed the workplace's "synthetic cubist" in no time!

Bring the cubist revolution to your cube with explosive colors and masterful artwork.

WALLS

■ The backdrop for this cube is simple and monotone, leaving breathing space for the cubist art. Select a color that will bring energy to your space—perhaps something bright, like yellow. Cut the colored vinyl to fit the cubicle walls and use straight pins to hold it at the top and bottom. (For tips on working with vinyl, see page 5.)

DESK

■ Select a shade of vinyl that complements the color of your cubicle walls. Cut the vinyl to cover the desk (leaving extra material to secure underneath with duct tape), and pull tight. If there are areas of the fabric that pull away from the desk around the perimeter, use double-sided tape for a clean finish.

A vividly colored rug will cover up bland industrial carpeting.

Use your cubist imagination to create a montage that would be at home in the Guggenheim or the Tate Modern.

Brightly colored office supplies have a myriad of uses.

■ Turn your desktop into a work of art itself with a collage of your favorite cubist art. Layer color copies of the art on your desk, overlapping the pieces. Once your masterpiece is complete, protect it with clear vinyl cut to fit the desk and secured underneath with duct tape.

DÉCOR

■ Your floor should make a statement, pulling the modern look together. If you can't find a rug similar to the one shown in the photo to the left, visit your local carpet remnants store and use a variety of multicolored scraps to create your own cubist-inspired rug.

■ Search for a lamp with a colored base that coordinates with your color scheme, or add a string of brightly colored lights along your wall.

■ Purchase a brightly colored guest chair to add to the vibrancy of your cube, and choose your office supplies in a variety of brilliant solid colors.

■ Hang reproductions of famous cubist art by Robert de la Fresnaye or Jacques Villon. If you'd rather make your own artwork, create a collage similar to the one on your desk and display it on your wall. Use double-sided tape to hang postcards or pictures on the vinyl wall.

■ Use miniature colored binder clips and pushpins to hang your favorite family photos. Use complementary colors, such as shades of green or another color you prefer.

■ Extend your color scheme to the treats you keep in your cube. A jumbo container of red licorice or a pen holder full of pinwheel lollipops adds color, and the treats will disappear fast. You can also leave out a bowl of colorful hard candy.

■ A shiny metal trash can will reflect the color from your carpet and cast vivid shades around your cube.

*zen*CUBE

Feng shui translates literally as "wind and water," two significant elements in nature. Several thousand years ago, the Chinese determined that these erosive forces should be considered when constructing homes and buildings. Today, the feng shui philosophy combines integrity, respect for the environment, and the use of nature's vitality to allow energy, or *chi*, to flow easily through all human surroundings. Design your cube to help you discover the virtue of balance and manifest your positive energy, wealth, health, and contentment.

Create a peaceful ambiance in your cube as you introduce the five elements to your work environment. A desktop water fountain with moss incorporates the Water and Earth elements; you can include the strong Metal element with a decorative wall hanging. Call up the spirit of Fire with lit candles, and the bamboo outlining your desk will complete the design with the Wood element. Your colleagues will gather to absorb the serenity of your work space and (gently) applaud your efforts.

A Zen cube will have you serenely chanting "Om" during even the most demanding times.

WALLS

■ Surround yourself with the Wood element by hanging corrugated paper printed with bamboo. Secure around the wall edges with straight pins or strips of Velcro.

■ Line the top of your cubicle with ¼-inch-wide (6.4 cm) bamboo. Use a hacksaw to cut each strip of bamboo. (Or, if possible, buy the bamboo precut, as it's difficult to cut yourself.) Then use hot glue to secure the strips to your walls. (For tips on working with hot glue, see page 5.)

DESK

■ Use natural fibers, such as burlap, to cover the desk and shelf. Cut the material to fit (leaving extra material to secure underneath with duct tape) and pull tight across the flat areas.

■ Use a hacksaw to cut more ¼-inch-wide (6.4 cm) strips of bamboo. Hot glue the strips to the natural material on the desk edges to accent the bamboo on the walls. Add natural raffia to the edges with hot glue to conceal any imperfections.

DÉCOR

■ Green accents are crucial when building your island of serenity. Place tall faux bamboo plants in each corner of your cubicle, or fill a white ceramic vase with bear grass, an attractive perennial wildflower you can find at most nurseries.

■ Natural fiber rugs, such as sisal, introduce another layer of serenity-inspiring depth.

■ Include a hand-carved wooden Buddha in your cube to bring peace on even the most stressful day.

■ Display a Zen sand garden next to your phone and rake away your worries during unending conference calls.

■ If you're able to light candles in your cubicle, put candles trimmed with bamboo on your desktop. If you can't find bamboo candles, cut small strips of bamboo, line them up around the perimeter of a large pillar candle, and tie with a natural-colored string to hold them in place.

■ Keep a lovely teapot on hand and share a cup of tea with a coworker on rainy days.

■ Choose a floor lamp with lantern-like shades in natural fibers to add depth to your cube.

■ Scour nurseries and home stores for the perfect copper fountain to bring the relaxing sounds of water to your cube. If the fountain is large enough, you can include rocks and moss or a fern for an earthy feel.

A fountain, a Zen garden, tins of feng shui candles representing each element, and a tea set on your desk will eliminate any negative energy.

*disco*CUBE

Disco never dies, so keep your disco ball spinning and your platform shoes shined! Whether it's the pulsating beats of techno or classic disco, the music we hate to love pervades our culture. Excessive times demand excessive decoration, so don't spare the glitz when conjuring up your disco cube. Adorn your standard desk chair with purple crushed velvet and knot it in the back for a decadent look. Rest a shimmery silver pillow on your guest chair so your coworkers can feel like they're exclusive guests at Studio 54. Bright, glimmering accessories, including the requisite disco ball, will complement the swanky velvet and shiny sequins. Crank up your iPod to keep the party hopping as you work so you'll be ready to hit the dance floor come Friday night.

Stay alive with the glimmer, shimmer, and sparkle of the dance floor.

Encourage dancing in your cube with a disco floor light show.

WALLS

■ Make your cubicle one giant disco ball by covering the walls with mirrored silver fabric. The fabric stretches, so you won't need quite as much as it appears when you first measure the walls. Cut the fabric to cover the entire surface and hang using plenty of straight pins on all the edges.

■ Trim the top and bottom of your walls with a 2-inch-wide (5 cm) ribbon of silver sequins, affixed to the fabric with straight pins or hot glue. (For tips on working with hot glue, see page 5.)

■ Cover shelves with silver vinyl and trim with strips from your silver wall covering, using hot glue to secure. (For tips on working with vinyl, see page 5.)

DESK

■ Silver vinyl is the perfect topper for a disco desk. Cut the vinyl to fit the top, leaving extra material to secure underneath, pull tight, and secure with duct tape.

■ Trim the desk with a silver fringe table skirt, and affix it to the vinyl with hot glue; line the top of the fringe with a 2-inch-wide (5 cm) strip of silver sequins.

Trim your wipe-off board with sequins for added glitz, and attach your favorite album cover or stills from Saturday Night Fever.

DÉCOR

■ Can you imagine dancing to Donna Summer's "Last Dance" without a disco ball? They're made in a variety of sizes, so mix it up. Hang a large disco ball in the center of your cube and place a smaller, revolving disco ball under your shelf. Use an even smaller disco ball as a paperweight.

■ Find quintessential seventies attire at your favorite vintage clothing store to add visual interest: Use a platform shoe as a bookend, or drape a white polyester coat over your guest chair. Place a glamorous set of shades on a foam mannequin head, add an Afro wig, and drape a bright feather boa around the mannequin's neck.

■ To create the effect of the lighted dance floor from *Saturday Night Fever*, purchase a color-changing mood light for your desk. Its shifting multicolored light replicates the glitzy patterns of the dance floor and can be timed to move slow or fast.

Top your mannequin head with a 'fro for a classic disco look.

■ Include the essential lava lamp to add color and enhance the seventies feel.

■ Your cube would be incomplete without a Studio 54 sign! Purchase matte board numbers, spray paint them black, and apply black glitter to each number with spray adhesive. Once the numbers are dry, hot glue the sign to the vinyl on your wall to welcome your guests.

*library*CUBE

Mahogany-paneled walls, a shuffling butler, silence in the reading room as smoke circles above late editions of the *Financial Times*—the private gentlemen's club maintains its allure in the minds of the uninvited. Create your own London club, like the famous White's or Boodles, and you'll be on your way toward fitting in among the upper echelons.

All great clubs begin with sumptuous, leather-backed chairs, easily acquired in a secondhand shop or antiques store. The aesthetic will speak volumes, as will a few classic books. Create a sense of history (and that nice, musty scent) with leather-bound tales of business or exploration. Need extra storage for office supplies? Try a humidor. Add some paneling, a standing globe, and a gilt-framed portrait of a one-time muckety-muck, and you'll have colleagues lining up to join your club.

Inflate your status in the company with this dignified, stately cube.

Fine accessories will add an old-money feel.

Cigar boxes and a humidor double as handy containers for office supplies.

WALLS

■ Creating a cubicle with a masculine look and feel begins with dark, luxurious materials—dark chocolate faux crocodile leather is ideal. Cover the cubicle walls from top to bottom in panels of this material. Use Velcro *and* straight pins to secure the material to the cubicle walls; it will be heavier than most vinyl. The deep color will help to create a seamless final presentation.

■ Cover shelves in the same faux crocodile leather, and cut a strip to trim the edge of the shelf as well, securing it in place with hot glue. (For tips on working with hot glue, see page 5.)

DESK

■ Cover the desk in a contrasting color of faux leather with a monochrome pattern to help to build the tone of masculinity. Cut the material to fit the desk, leaving extra to secure underneath with duct tape, and pull it tight.

DÉCOR

■ An oversized painted portrait, preferably of a distinguished-looking gentleman framed in gold, is the cornerstone for this design. Think of the founding fathers of the classic private gentlemen's clubs and scour flea markets and antique stores to find the perfect portrait. A serious expression is a must.

■ A brass or wood coat rack is a perfect place to hang your coat. Add a silk scarf and a derby hat for a sophisticated touch.

■ Layering your cubicle with stacks of old books flanked by vintage bookends creates the old-world feeling that is essential to this cube. The top of a stack of books is also a great spot to

Keep brandy (or iced tea) and cigars on hand for when the boys stop by.

place a prop or two (such as an ashtray for your cigar), giving height to some of your more prized possessions.

■ Company rules may prevent you from serving brandy to guests, but a crystal or etched decanter placed on your desk can be filled with iced tea on a hot afternoon.

■ A gentlemen's club would not be complete without cigars. Whether you have actual cigars on hand to give to your coworkers or chocolate cigars to enjoy during a late afternoon meeting, a box of stogies will really help to set the tone.

■ Although open flames may be against office policy, a brass candlestick with a candle helps to create ambiance even without a light.

■ For a classic touch, add the green glow of a library lamp.

■ A standing globe provides a reference point for stories about your travels or a place for you to plot new adventures.

■ Store your paper clips or tacks in a vintage wood ashtray for another unique touch.

*ice*CUBE

Haven't trekked to Antarctica in a few winters? You can capture the essence of that white wonderland by putting your work environment in a deep freeze. A work space wrapped in chill will draw coworkers over for a breath of refreshing air.

Accenting your cube with winter's veil requires that you fashion every accoutrement in the hue of a snow hare. The walls should look like a snow-blanketed winter landscape. Adding white fringe and faux ice cubes to office supplies and penguin stewards upon designated floes will enhance the chilly effect, and a few large ice cube lights will offer cool and creative ambiance. Ensconced in a world of icy white and snow-capped trees, you'll be the center of attention when it's time to chill in the office. Don't forget to turn the thermostat up, 'cause, baby, it's cold inside!

Experience the refreshing vistas of the Arctic without the freezing temperatures, windchill, and ice.

project: ICY OFFICE SUPPLIES

MATERIALS:

- Acrylic in-box
- Pencil and pen holders
- Containers to hold paper-clips and rubber bands
- White paper fringe
- Hot glue gun
- Hot glue
- Acrylic ice cubes

1. Trim the edge of the top and bottom of each container in a white paper fringe, using hot glue to attach it to the acrylic.

2. Nestle acrylic ice cubes (found at a party store) throughout the paper fringe and secure them with a touch of hot glue on the bottom of each cube.

WALLS

■ Construct your winter wonderland by covering the walls with an image that creates the feel of a deep freeze. Corrugated paper decorated with a landscape of snow-capped trees sets the scene. Hang it on the walls using Velcro strips and straight pins on the top, bottom, and sides of your wall.

■ Let it snow! Place strips of cotton batting on your cubicle floor along the perimeter. Pull the batting in several places so it stretches up about a foot (30 cm) of the wall, secure to the corrugated paper with hot glue, and sprinkle faux snow throughout. (For tips on working with hot glue, see page 5.) Placing the batting only at the perimeter, in low traffic areas, ensures the mess will be minimal.

■ Add a border of corrugated icicles to the top of the cubicle walls, using straight pins to hold them in place.

■ White paper fringe separating the snow scene from the cotton batting will add texture and definition, while miniature white ice cubes applied to the fringe add a whimsical touch. Use hot glue to attach both elements.

■ Cover the shelves in white vinyl, using hot glue to secure it. (For tips on working with vinyl, see page 5.) Trim the shelves in the white paper fringe to coordinate with the walls.

DESK

■ The key to this cube is keeping horizontal surfaces white to create a chilly look and feel, so use white vinyl to cover the desk. Cut the vinyl to fit the top of the desk (leaving extra material to secure underneath), pull tight, and secure to the desk with duct tape.

■ Purchase a white plastic fringe table skirt from your local party supply store and cut it to the length of your desk. Hot glue to the edge of the desk. Hot glue white paper fringe to the top of the desk edge. Attach miniature white acrylic ice

Cool peppermint patties and chilly-looking treats are good snacks, and the glass containers will evoke the appearance of ice.

Add a group of faux pine trees in the corner of your cube, and toss a bag of faux snow at them to settle throughout their branches.

To replicate ice sculptures, search for clear, ice blue votive candleholders or vases; they look realistic and add a wet, glossy accent to your cube.

Your coworkers will thank you as they dig into your clear glass jars filled with a mixture of silver and white treats. Yogurt-covered raisins, chocolate kisses, and especially chilly peppermint patties are good choices.

To complete the look, use office supplies in chrome or white.

Place ice cube lights on the floor and your desk to enhance the white interior and brighten up drab carpeting.

An Antarctic penguin reminds you to keep cool during even the most stressful days.

cubes throughout the paper fringe with hot glue for added dimension.

DÉCOR

What ice cube would be complete without penguins waddling through your office space or resting on the nearest floe? Whether you add one or a whole flock, plastic penguins will be sure to make your coworkers chuckle and add cheer to your workdays.

RESOURCES

Archie McPhee (www.mcphee.com)
Bed Bath & Beyond (www.bedbathandbeyond.com)
Cost Plus World Market (www.worldmarket.com)
Display & Costume (www.displaycostume.com)
eParty Unlimited (www.epartyunlimited.com)
Home Depot (www.homedepot.com)
IKEA (www.ikea.com)

Pacific Fabrics and Crafts (www.pacificfabrics.com)
Plum Party (www.plumparty.com)
Restoration Hardware (www.restorationhardware.com)
Staples (www.staples.com)
Target (www.target.com)
Uncommon Goods (www.uncommongoods.com)

■ SAFARI CUBE

Cost Plus World Market: wooden ladder, wooden chest, African mask, wooden giraffes, desk lamp, faux banana plant, carved gourds, capiz shell curtains
Bed Bath & Beyond: clock/picture frame
Display & Costume: feather wall trim, faux fur desk trim, safari hat
Pacific Fabrics and Crafts: burlap wall covering

■ GARDEN CUBE

Archie McPhee: pastel weave desk covering
Display & Costume: silk wisteria wall trim, cobblestone corrugated paper, grosgrain ribbon, desk trim, faux grass wall covering, blue ribbon
eParty Unlimited: miniature horseshoe set
IKEA: white mushroom, mini watering can, Astroturf circle
Plum Party: squirrel topiary
Ravenna Gardens (www.ravennagardens.com): scroll lantern, urns, bird bath, garden umbrella
Target: silk hydrangeas, leather desk accessories, glass carafe

■ MOD CUBE

Archie McPhee: wall covering, desk trim
Design Within Reach (www.designwithinreach.com): Utensilo wall organizer

Display & Costume: white vinyl wall covering
IKEA: red mod picture, white light, red carpet circles
Target: leather desk accessories

■ GLAM CUBE

Daly's Paint and Decorating Wood Finishes (www.dalyspaint.com): wallpaper
Display & Costume: mini Oscars, fringe desk trim, boas, Marilyn Monroe cutout, maroon velour desk covering
Lucca Statuary (www.luccastatuary.com): reproduction film posters

■ TIKI CUBE

Archie McPhee: wood-grain oil cloth, bamboo, Tiki eraser heads, surfer
Cost Plus World Market: faux palm tree
Display & Costume: table hula skirt, faux silk orchids, faux algae, ocean corrugated paper, blue corrugated paper, manzanita branches
Hawaiian General Store (www.hawaiiangeneralstore.net): Tiki gods, float ball, palm mat
Velocity Art & Design (www.velocityartanddesign.com): Jonathan Adler pottery
Uncommon Goods: blue office supply holder
You can find additional Tiki paraphernalia at sites like eBay, www.hawaiiankinestuff.com, and www.paradisefound.com.

■ PUB CUBE

Cost Plus World Market: beer steins
Display & Costume: wood-grain corrugated paper, natural corrugated paper, brown felt
eParty Unlimited: miniature pool table
Plum Party: beer coasters
Target: wooden desk accessories

■ NAP CUBE

Cooking.com (www.cooking.com): dry goods/cereal dispenser
Cost Plus World Market: cream dispenser
Design Within Reach (www.designwithinreach.com): white Bubble Club chair
Display & Costume: stars, white netting, white cotton batting
Uncommon Goods: white office supply holder

■ INDIA CUBE

Cost Plus World Market: saris, brass accessories, rod iron candle holders, red wooden bench, beaded lamp, tea glasses
Display & Costume: gold lamé desk and shelf covering, red desk trim

■ GOLF CUBE

Display & Costume: Astroturf, green felt
Home Depot: chicken wire
Target: putting game

Restoration Hardware: leather chair
Uncommon Goods: golfer bank

■ NYC CUBE
Bed Bath & Beyond: paper shredder
Display & Costume: yellow vinyl desk covering, black vinyl, checkerboard ribbon trim
Just Murals (www.justmurals.com): Manhattan mural
Restoration Hardware: Brooklyn Bridge bookends
Toy Destination (www.toyd.com): checkered cabs
Uncommon Goods: taxicab medallion clock

■ CABIN CUBE
Burnt Sugar (601 N. 35th St.; Seattle, WA 98103; 206-545-0699): dog statue
Display & Costume: faux birch, suede ribbon, fall leaves corrugated paper
REI (www.rei.com): lantern, Nalgene bottle
Target: s'more maker

■ COLLECTOR'S CUBE
Apple (www.apple.com): iPod, iPod speakers
Archie McPhee: pom-pom fringe, fuchsia and white polka dot desk and shelf covering
Display & Costume: fuchsia wall and desk covering, white vinyl wall covering
Funko (www.funko.com): bobble heads
IKEA: clock, white plastic chair
Target: mercury lamp, bathroom set

■ C.E.O. CUBE
Annie's Art (2212 NW Market St.; Seattle, WA 98107; 206-784-4761): skyline poster
Display & Costume: gray velour desk covering, maroon velour desk covering
Home Depot: crown molding
Staples: metal desk accessories

■ CASINO CUBE
Archie McPhee: gold vinyl desk covering
Display & Costume: gold table curtain, gold sequin trim, felt game table
Lyons Antique Mall (4516 California Ave. SW; Seattle, WA 98116; 206-935-9774): gold mask with feathers
Overstock.com (www.overstock.com): Automatic Skill Stop slot machine
Spencer Gifts (www.spencergifts.com): neon dealer sign
Toy Destination (www.toyd.com): "Welcome to Fabulous Las Vegas" sign

■ ROCK CUBE
Apple (www.apple.com): iPod, iPod speakers
Display & Costume: zebra fabric wall covering, tie-dye mesh wall covering, red vinyl wall covering, flame ribbon
IKEA: faux fur rug
Rock Memories (2525 6th Ave.; Seattle, WA 98121; 206-448-1262): reproduction rock posters, Rolling Stone mouse pad, Pink Floyd mug
Uncommon Goods: orange office supply holder

■ SCI-FI CUBE
Archie McPhee: lightbulb light
Display & Costume: alien mask, black metallic mesh
eParty Unlimited: Lumin Disk
IKEA: white plastic chair
Pacific Fabric and Crafts: chalk cloth
Uncommon Goods: robot clock

■ HIP-HOP CUBE
Display & Costume: faux stone spray paint, faux boulders, rope lights, faux bling, industrial piping, foam trim, spray paint
IKEA: gray suede shag rug

■ CUBISM CUBE
Annie's Art (2212 NW Market St.; Seattle, WA 98107; 206-784-4761): cubism posters
Display & Costume: clear vinyl desk covering, yellow vinyl, red vinyl wall covering
eParty Unlimited: watercolor lights
IKEA: abstract rug, blue plastic chair, blue plastic lamp
Staples: colored binder clips and pushpins

■ ZEN CUBE
Bed Bath & Beyond: bamboo candle
Cost Plus World Market: faux bamboo, hanging lanterns, bamboo ladder, black metal desk accessories, jute rug, wooden Buddha, feng shui candles
Display & Costume: bamboo corrugated paper
eParty Unlimited: Zen garden
IKEA: white ceramic vase
Pacific Fabrics and Crafts: burlap desk covering

■ DISCO CUBE
Apple (www.apple.com): iPod, iPod speakers.
Champion Party Supply (www.championpartysupply.com): purple velvet hat, feather boa
Display & Costume: disco balls, silver table skirt, silver sequins, cardboard numbers, mask, wig
eParty Unlimited: lava lamp

■ LIBRARY CUBE
Bed Bath & Beyond: lamp
Pacific Galleries Antique Mall (www.pacgal.com): portrait of man
Plum Party: chocolate cigars
Restoration Hardware: leather chair

■ ICE CUBE
Archie McPhee: plastic penguins
Display & Costume: white table skirt, cotton batting, corrugated icicle, corrugated winter scene
IKEA: ice cube lights
Packaging Specialties (www.pkgspec.com): fun fringe
Staples: acrylic office supplies

ACKNOWLEDGMENTS

One of my favorite quotes is George Bernard Shaw's: "Life isn't about finding yourself, it's about creating yourself." I am blessed to have amazing people in my life who have helped me to create a life that at one time I could only dream of. I would like to thank my mom and dad for loving me so deeply and supporting me in whatever crazy endeavor I have wanted to pursue. Thank you also to Tiffany Sharer McGehee for your friendship and for inspiring me to see my talent and value myself. To Nikki Mundie Putnam and Kathy McQuaid for working so hard and keeping a smile on your faces—despite the glue-gun burns. To Crai Bower for understanding my passion and helping me put that passion into words. To Sheena Spicer Kalso for measuring and cutting yards of fabric. To Kyla Johnson for the caffeine to get us through it all, and for the extra set of hands. To James Knoblich for loaning me your shoulder to cry on when I couldn't see the light at the end of the tunnel. To Rachel Hart, Lisa Youngblood Hall, Kate Anderson, and Lou Maxon for mentoring me and teaching me so much despite your busy schedules. To Ali Bayse for thinking of me for this project. To Adrienne Wiley and Kate Perry for your flexibility and willingness to cover shelves. To Todd Bates for your eye and an amazing layout. To Justin Gollmar for capturing a cube exactly as I imagined in record time. And finally, to my dear friends Nisha Kelen, Chelsea Hixon, Cassie LaValle, Mike Kicherer, Jason Dodd, John Butigan, Curtis and Paul Hannum, and Joyce Shannahan for believing in me and inviting me into your world.